You Can't Send a Duck to Eagle School

And Other Simple Truths of **Leadership**

MAC ANDERSON

simple **truths**
LEAD TO CHANGE

an imprint of Sourcebooks, Inc.

Photo Credits
Cover and internals © Scott Anderson; VectorState

Published by Simple Truths, an imprint of Sourcebooks, Inc.
P.O. Box 4410, Naperville, Illinois 60567-4410
(630) 961-3900
Fax: (630) 961-2168
www.sourcebooks.com

Originally published in 2006 in the United States of America by Simple Truths.

Printed and bound in the United States of America.
WOZ 10 9 8 7 6 5 4 3 2

Contents

Introduction

I once had lunch with a top executive from a company known for their legendary retail service. My wife and I are both huge fans, and over lunch I shared with him some of the great service stories his people had provided the Anderson family. I said, "With the service your people give, you must have a training manual two inches thick."

He looked up and said, "Mac, we don't have a training manual. What we do is find the best people we can find, and we empower them to do whatever it takes to satisfy the customer." Then he said something I'll never forget: "We learned a long time ago that you can't send a duck to eagle school."

"Excuse me?" I asked.

He repeated, "You can't send a duck to eagle school." He said, "You can't teach someone to smile; you can't teach someone to want to serve; you can't teach personality. What we can do, however, is hire people who have those qualities, and we can then teach them about our products and teach them our culture."

As long as I live, I will never forget this simple analogy about hiring people.

It is branded on my brain forever. And since that day, with every hiring decision I've made, I find myself asking this question: "Am I hiring a duck, thinking they will become an eagle?" I can honestly say that asking this simple question has saved me from making some important hiring mistakes.

I just wish I'd heard it twenty years sooner.

The "duck to eagle school" lesson is one of many simple truths of leadership that I've learned on my journey as an entrepreneur. In the past thirty years, I've had the good fortune to be involved with three successful start-up companies, each becoming a leader in its niche. And, as you can imagine, there have been many peaks, valleys, and lessons learned along the way.

I've also been very fortunate to have met a lot of people who are a lot smarter than I am. Successful entrepreneurs, authors, speakers, educators, coaches, and CEOs of large companies have all helped shape my thinking. It has been their wisdom and their knowledge, combined with my own life experiences, that have helped shape who I am today.

My goal with this book is to share some of my lessons learned in a brief but engaging way. Because so many times it's not what is said but how it is said that turns the switch from off to on. For me, one of the most exciting things about business and life is that one great idea can change our lives forever.

All the best,

Mac Anderson

Founder, Simple Truths and Successories

Leadership Would Be Easy, If It Wasn't for People

There is one question that every employee will love to have you ask: What can I do to help? So many times as leaders, we assume we're doing all we can do; however, these six words—What can I do to help?—will usually prove your assumptions are dead wrong. The question should address three areas:

1. What can I do to help you serve the customer better?
2. What can I do to make your working environment more pleasant?
3. What can I do to help you better balance your work and family life?

Obviously, it's important to let them know up front that you may not be able to help with everything they ask, but you'll do what you can. In other words, a chauffeur to and from work is probably out of the question.

You'll usually be amazed to hear about a few small things that will cost you next to nothing. You may find their chair is uncomfortable or they need a new file cabinet, flex hours one day a week, a new headset for the phone, or a small space heater in the winter months. The truth is, the fact that you've taken the time to listen to their personal concerns is far more important in their eyes than what you'll do for them. Gallup polled over one million employees who thought they had a great boss and asked them one question: Why? You got it! The number one reason was the boss was willing to listen to what they had to say. Never forget: it's the little things, not the big ones, that will earn the respect of your people.

"Listening is wanting to hear."

—*Jim Cathcart*

Change Is Good...
You Go First

A while back Tom Feltenstein said, "Mac, we should write a book together, and the title could be *Change Is Good... You Go First*." I immediately loved the idea, and we added the subtitle "21 Ways to Inspire Change."

Change is the key that unlocks the door to growth and excitement in any organization. The leader's ability to inspire a culture of change can make or break their success. Tomorrow comes at us with lightning speed, and our competitive advantage is a fleeting thing. Bill Gates puts it this way: "In three years, every product my company makes will be obsolete. The only question is whether we will make them obsolete or somebody else will." Peter Drucker reinforced what Gates said by saying, "Every three years, each product and process should be put on trial for its life; otherwise, the competition will pass you by." Drucker also says that most companies find it easier to come up with new ideas than to let go of old ones.

Have you ever watched a fly bouncing off a window pane, even with an open door a few feet away? Many times the fly keeps crashing into the glass until it finally dies. There are many companies in today's world doing exactly the same thing. They continue down today's path, wearing blinders to the possibility of change—until they die.

Keeping change and continuous improvements on the front burner is never easy. We are so focused on today's problems that we put off planning for tomorrow's opportunities.

Keeping change alive starts with rewarding innovation, risk taking, and creativity. In fact, you need to fail quickly and fail often to stay ahead of the competition. T. S. Eliot said it best: "Only those who will risk going too far can possibly find out how far one can go."

"In the end,
it is important to
remember that we
cannot become
what we need to
be by remaining
who we are."

—*Max De Pree*

Accept Your Limitations and You'll Expand Your Potential

One of the biggest reasons many leaders fail is their unwillingness to accept their limitations. Ego gets in the way. They feel they're smart enough to do it all and mistakenly feel that what they don't know can be learned on the fly. So many times it's a recipe for disaster, especially for entrepreneurs.

Walt Disney failed many times early in his career. He had brilliant ideas, but his ability to execute them was painfully lacking. He also, believe it or not, was a lousy artist. After the third failure, Disney was finally convinced that, to succeed, he must surround himself with great artists who could bring his animation ideas to life. He also needed his brother, Roy, to handle the financial side of the business. These two moves made all the difference and freed Walt up to do what he did best—using his imagination to plan their future.

I can definitely relate to the Disney story. From 1991 to 1993, we were on a roll at Successories. We had gone from $5 million to $45 million in three years. Then came 1994, and Murphy's Law hit us like a ton of bricks. We had grown too fast and no longer had the right people or infrastructure to handle it. Early in 1995, I realized that I had to make significant changes. After a lot of soul searching, I realized my strengths were people skills and creativity; however, my weaknesses were operations and accounting. To grow the business and rebuild the infrastructure, I had to hire good people who had been there and done that, people who could complement what I did best. This was a very painful wake-up call, but I learned some of the most valuable lessons of my life.

I once heard a quote that offers every manager and entrepreneur food for thought:

"If your company mission is to climb a tree, which would you rather do: hire a squirrel or train a horse?"

Forget Real Good...
Remember Feel Good

I met Tom Asacker at a conference in Hawaii where we both spoke. There was one thing he said that I never forgot. He said as leaders we need to "forget real good and remember feel good."

Today, he said, there are billions of web pages and more going up every day. He once saw eighty-nine brands of shampoo at Walgreens!

Customers are stressed out from information overload and conflicting information. More and more they are relying on their gut—and their feelings—to make decisions.

In fact, he said, it really doesn't matter how customers feel about you and your business. What makes a difference is how your products make them feel about themselves and their decisions. Every psychologist and smart marketer knows that if people do something and it feels good, they'll do it again; if it feels bad, they won't.

Far too many companies are focused on the product and not the experience. We need to replace our brain with our heart, because that's often how people make decisions. Studies have proven that the essential difference between emotion and reason is that emotion leads to action and reason leads to conclusions.

What do you want? Do you want action, or do you want people to think?

The question you need to ask is "How am I making my customers feel?"

Am I making them compare or care? There's a big difference. Caring and feelings drive action; the other stuff is just a tool. The bottom line is that the really hard stuff is the soft stuff: it's the feelings of your employees and customers.

That, in the end, is your competitive advantage.

"If you throw your heart over the fence, the rest will follow."

—*Anonymous*

Attitude Isn't Everything, but It's Pretty Darn Close

When hiring someone, start with the premise that attitudes are contagious. Then ask yourself one question: **Is theirs worth catching?**

I've been in business for over thirty years, and I've come to realize the difference in success and failure is not how you look, not how you dress, not how much you're educated, but **how you think!**

In my business life, I've watched many very intelligent people fail miserably because they have a negative attitude, and I've also observed just as many people with average intelligence soar to success because of positive attitudes.

Southwest Airlines's vice president of people is often asked the question **"How do you get your people to be so nice?"** Her answer is always the same: **"We hire nice people."**

It sounds almost too simple to feel important, but

hiring nice people has been the cornerstone of their amazing success in a highly competitive industry. They understand their competitors may be able to match their price and copy their business model; however, they feel that the spirit and the attitude of their employees will be extremely difficult to replicate. Never forget: great customer service is only delivered by nice, passionate, caring employees. There is no other way it can happen.

"Customer service is not a department. It's an attitude."

—*Anonymous*

The Road to Success Is Not Always a Road

One of my favorite books is *Paper Airplane*, written by my good friend Michael McMillan, whom I consider a creative genius—and I rarely use the *G* word. Michael has the unique ability to bring simple ideas to life in an unforgettable way.

The subtitle, "A Lesson for Flying Outside the Box," is something very difficult for most leaders to do. However, history proves that creative breakthroughs in science, technology, and business only occur when people challenge the accepted norm and take action. Innovation comes from leaving the proven map behind to explore new territories.

In *Paper Airplane*, Michael shares how his sixth-grade teacher, Mrs. Hackett, spent the entire week teaching the class aerodynamics. To complete the lesson, she organized a paper airplane contest. The kids were given a sheet of construction paper and fifteen minutes to build a winning plane.

They all went to work carefully folding their paper, hoping to create a plane that would travel the farthest. Before long, everyone was ready to go outside to start the contest…or nearly everyone. Jeff, a unique young man who marched to the beat of a different drum, hadn't made one fold in his paper. He was staring out the window, thinking. To give him a little more time, Mrs. Hackett told Jeff he could go last.

The contest was interesting on many levels. Some of the planes barely flew five feet while others did surprisingly well. One thing was certain—the line was thinning down, and Jeff was still holding a flat piece of construction paper.

Before long, Jeff was the only remaining contestant. With great anticipation, the class watched as Jeff approached with his craft hidden behind his back. Then he stepped to the line and exposed his masterpiece—a flat sheet of paper. As the class started to snicker, Jeff confidently wadded up the paper into a ball and threw it farther than the leading plane had flown. The crowd went wild!

Michael explains that Jeff demonstrated a new way of interpreting a problem and had the courage to act on his vision. He's never said, but I've always suspected Jeff's real name might be Michael.

One of my favorite quotes that hangs on my office wall is: "You cannot discover new oceans unless you have the courage to lose sight of the shore."

You Only Get One Chance to Make a Good Impression

Some years ago I had dinner with a friend and met his wife, Terri, for the first time. Our dinner conversation led to the fact that I had started McCord Travel, and she said, "I can't believe it! I used to work for McCord." She then said, "I have wonderful memories of my time at McCord, and I'll never forget how they treated me my first day on the job."

I sold McCord in 1985, and my friend, Bruce Black, stayed on to run the company for the new owner, so I can take no credit for Terri's special memory.

Terri said, "There was something different happening from the moment I walked through the front door, more energy and more smiles than I was used to at other jobs. I was greeted by a very nice young lady who said she was going to be my mentor during the first week, and if I had any questions, she'd be happy to answer them.

She introduced me to the people in each department. At lunch she presented me with a gift of personalized stationery. They all went the extra mile to make me feel at home…and I'll never forget it."

Robert W. Baird, an employee-owned investment company from Milwaukee, was listed by *Forbes Magazine* as one of the hundred best companies to work for. They believe in the personal touch. New hires are greeted with flowers on their desk, and they also meet with the CEO for a new associates event. The company understands that little things can make a big difference.

Another first impression idea is to send a note and a small gift to the employee's home, welcoming them on board. This way, the employee's spouse (if they're married) is left with a good first impression as well.

Most leaders grossly underestimate the power of a first impression, not only of their employees, but also of their customers. For example, Marj Webber was my assistant at Successories. Among other duties, Marj was responsible for dealing with the various photography companies we used for our prints, cards, etc. One day she came into my office and said, "I've been doing this for a long time, but this is the nicest letter I've ever received." She said she had just placed an order with Alaska Stock Images and received this letter a few days later. Here's what it said:

> Dear Marjorie,
>
> Thank you for your recent purchase. We appreciate the opportunity to serve you and look forward to working with you again. We hope you'll enjoy the enclosed gift.
>
> Satisfied customers are our best advertisement, so I encourage you to give us feedback on how we're doing. If we ever disappoint you, I hope you'll let us know; we'll do everything we can to make things right.
>
> In the meantime, if you have any questions or require assistance, please feel free to contact us.
>
> Thank you again for selecting us. It is our privilege to work with you.
>
> Sincerely,
> Laurie Campbell, Alaska Stock Images

Now, tell me: How long did it take to write this letter and send a small gift? The answer is not long! But the impact was powerful and lasting. It immediately separated this vendor from the competition.

Never forget: with every new employee and every new customer, you have only one chance—just one—to make a great first impression. Plan it. Make it all it can be!

"Giving people a
little more than
they expect is a
good way to get
back a lot more
than you'd expect."

—*Robert Half*

Eat That Frog

There's an old saying that says, "If the first thing you do when you wake up in the morning is eat a live frog, then nothing worse can happen for the rest of the day!" Well, I don't know about you, but I think that's a pretty safe assumption.

Brian Tracy, in his book *Eat That Frog*, says that your "frog" should be the most difficult item on your to-do list, the one where you're most likely to procrastinate, because if you eat that first, it'll give you energy and momentum for the rest of the day. But if you don't, and you let him sit there on the plate and stare at you while you do a hundred unimportant things, it can drain your energy and you won't even know it.

So here's your assignment: for the next thirty days, take a look at your list, circle the frog, and eat that first.

You'll thank me for it.

"PROCRASTINATION
is attitude's
natural assassin.

There's nothing so fatiguing as an uncompleted task."

—*William James*

Less Is Almost Always More

Two of the all-time greatest coaches in sports history were Red Auerbach, who coached the great Boston Celtics basketball team in the 1950s and '60s, and Vince Lombardi, the legendary football coach for the Green Bay Packers. When I read their biographies, what struck me most was their keep-it-simple philosophy. While other coaches were teaching complicated offense and defense, both Lombardi and Auerbach only had a few plays, but this was the key—they executed the plays to perfection.

Someone once asked Auerbach what magic formula he had for winning games. He laughed and said, "Our secret to success is what I would call 'effective simplicity.' Nothing complicated. In fact, we only have seven different plays, and Bill Russell touched the ball on every one of them."

Under Auerbach's effective simplicity philosophy, the Boston Celtics won every championship from 1959 through 1966—eight years in a row, a record unmatched since.

Lombardi's coaching philosophy was strikingly similar, and he had only five running plays in his offense but, like Auerbach, executed every play to perfection. He'd often say, "We really don't fool anyone. The opposition knows what's coming, but they rarely stop us because every player knows his assignment, and we've practiced it a thousand times."

Lombardi was fanatical when it came to teaching and reinforcing the basic fundamentals of the game. In his mind, blocking and tackling were the keys to winning football games. In fact, to make his point on fundamentals, every year he would begin his training camp by saying, "Gentlemen, this is a football."

"Winning is not a sometime thing; it is an all the time thing. You don't win once in a while; you don't do things right once in a while; you do them right all of the time."

—*Vince Lombardi*

Get a Second Job

You may have heard this Ralph Waldo Emerson quote: "The speed of the leader determines the rate of the pack." Well, here's another one for you: "The attitude of the leader determines the attitude of the pack."

Because I'm the founder of Successories, some people think that this guy probably never has a negative thought. How wrong they would be! Like every human being, I have doubts, fears, and disappointments in my life. As a leader, however, we must manage our attitudes. Do we need to be perfect? Of course not. But we can never underestimate the influence that our actions and our attitudes will have on our team. Winston Churchill said, "The price of greatness is responsibility," and part of that responsibility is to stay positive whether you feel like it or not.

Managing your attitude is a very personal thing. For me, however, the most important factor is exercise. My attitude and my energy levels are directly tied to exercise. I can be doing everything else right, but without regular exercise, I can feel my attitude heading south.

I have a friend who, at sixty-five, looked like he was fifty-five. When I saw him, I said, "Tony, you look great."

He said, "I feel great! I got a second job."

I said, "A second job? I thought your import business was doing well."

He said, "It is. My second job is on the treadmill from six to seven every morning. When I started looking at it as a second job, I showed up whether I wanted to or not! The pay is lousy, but the benefits to my health and my attitude are priceless!"

Exercise, more than anything, is a stress buster. And don't kid yourself: stress is a killer. A Carnegie Mellon research team showed that the effects of psychological stress on the body's ability to regulate inflammation can promote the development and progression of disease. Therefore, if you're not proactive in busting stress, it's very likely to come back and bust you!

"Change your
thoughts and
you change
your world."

—*Norman Vincent Peale*

Wisdom Is Knowing the Right Path to Take… Integrity Is Taking It

The dictionary defines *integrity* as "the quality or state of being complete or undivided." Simply put, when you have integrity, your words and your deeds match up.

John C. Maxwell says, "Integrity is not what we do so much as who we are. And who we are, in turn, determines what we do." Even Socrates reminds us, "The first key to greatness is to be in reality what we appear to be."

Integrity is never easy, but most of all, it requires self-discipline, inner trust, and honesty at all times. The poem "Myself" by Edgar Guest is on the next page. Keep it handy, and read it often!

Myself

I have to live with myself and so
I want to be fit for myself to know,
I want to be able as days go by,
Always to look myself straight in the eye;
I don't want to stand with the setting sun
And hate myself for the things I've done.

I don't want to keep on a closet shelf
A lot of secrets about myself,
And fool myself as I come and go
Into thinking no one else will ever know
The kind of person I really am;
I don't want to dress up myself in sham.

I want to go out with my head erect,
I want to deserve all men's respect;
But here in this struggle for fame and pelf
I want to be able to like myself.
I don't want to look at myself and know
That I am a bluster and bluff and empty show.

I never can hide myself from me;
I see what others may never see;
I know what others may never know,
I never can fool myself and so,

Whatever happens, I want to be
Self-respecting and conscience free.

—Edgar Guest

Define Your Moment of Truth

In 1982, Jan Carlzon had just been named the CEO of Scandinavian Airlines. His company was in trouble. They had just been ranked by a consumer poll as the worst airline in the world. Last in service, last in dependability, and last in profits as a percentage of sales. Yet one year later, in the same poll, they were ranked number one in all three categories.

What happened?

Carlzon had decided to focus on what he thought was the most critical issue: serving the customer. He wanted to keep it simple. Identify every contact between the customer and the employee, and treat that contact as "a moment of truth."

He set out to let his people know the importance of that moment—the captain, the ticket agent, the baggage handler, the flight attendant.

"Every moment, every contact," he said, "must be as pleasant and as memorable as possible."

He figured that he had approximately ten million customers each year, and on average, each customer made contact with five of his people for approximately fifteen seconds apiece. Therefore, in his mind, these fifty million contacts, fifteen seconds at a time, would determine the fate of his company.

He set out to share his vision with his twenty thousand employees. He knew the key was to empower the front line. Let them make the decision and take action, because they were Scandinavian Airlines during those fifteen seconds. He now had twenty thousand people who were energized and ready to go because they were focused on one very important thing—making every moment count.

"A leader's job is to look into the future and see the organization, not as it is, but as it should be."

—*Jack Welch*

Companies Don't Succeed...People Do

To build a customer-first culture, you must put them second. Your employees must come first, because there is a rule of thumb in business that says, "Your people will only treat your customers as well as they are being treated. Thus, to have satisfied customers, they must be served by passionate people."

Howard Schultz, the founder of Starbucks, is one of my favorite leaders. His book *Pour Your Heart into It* is excellent. In it, he offers in great detail all the obstacles he overcame in turning his vision into reality.

Early on, Schultz realized that the key to his success was to recruit well-educated people who were eager to communicate his passion for coffee. This, he felt, would be his competitive advantage in an industry where turnover was 300 percent a year. To hire the best people, he also knew he must be willing to pay them more than the going wage and offer health benefits that weren't available elsewhere. He saw that part-time people made up two-thirds of his employee base, and no one in the restaurant industry offered benefits to part-timers.

Schultz went to work in an effort to sell his board of directors on increasing expenses while most restaurant executives in the 1980s were looking for ways to cut costs. Initially, Schultz's pleas to investors and the board fell on deaf ears, because Starbucks was still losing money. But Schultz was persistent. He was looking long term and was committed to growing the business with passionate people. He won and said many times afterward that this decision was one of the most important decisions, if not the most important, that he made at Starbucks. His employee retention rate was about five times the industry average, but more importantly, he attracted people with great attitudes who made their customers feel welcome and at home.

Over the years, Schultz often showed how much he cared for his people. Early on July 7, 1997, he and his family were asleep at home in East Hampton, New York.

The phone rang, and he learned that three Starbucks employees had been murdered in a botched robbery in Washington, DC. A stunned Schultz immediately chartered a plane and arrived there before nine that morning. He stayed for a week, working with the police, meeting with the victims' families, and attending funerals. He ultimately decided that the future profits of the store would go to organizations working for violence prevention and victims' rights.

Howard Schultz gets it. A common quote of the Starbucks team tells it all:

"We aren't in the coffee business, serving people. We're in the people business, serving coffee."

Expect to Win

One of my favorite things to do at work is read letters or emails from customers who share their stories about how our products have made a positive difference in their lives or in their businesses. It makes me feel great.

One day, I got a letter from Mark Wilkerson, an executive for a major insurance company. One of our gift books inspired Mark to tell a story about how something his dad told him as a child had shaped his life. I'm sharing it with you because I think it's wonderful advice for any leader.

When Mark was growing up, he loved baseball, and his dad was the coach of his Little League baseball team. He remembered his dad saying repeatedly, "Prepare for each play and know what to do with the baseball if it is hit to you. I want all of you to want the ball to be hit to you!"

His dad said, "Look over your options. Decide what you should do, take a deep breath, and let it out; raise up on your toes to be ready and say to yourself, 'Hit the ball to me!' Then if you make the play, be humble. If you make an error, put it behind you and keep doing the same thing on every pitch."

At the end of Mark's letter, he wrote, "Mr. Anderson, I want to share a poem with you that I wrote when my dad died in 1988."

His poem certainly inspired me, and with Mark's permission, I'm honored to share it with you.

Thanks, Dad: A Tribute

When our team is in the field,
The other at the plate—
The last half inning to be played,
One play will seal our fate.

Bases are loaded; there are two outs.
We've fought to get this far—
The pressure high, adrenaline flowing—
Our record could be marred.

Expect to Win

We're ahead by just one run.
It's very close you see—
This is the point where most folks say,
"Don't hit the ball to me."

Encouraged and taught to trust myself,
With confidence by Dad—
In opportunity there is no losing,
Just lessons to be had.

So I take a breath and ask myself,
"What if it comes my way?"
I make the decision to smile and say,
"Hit the ball to me. I can make the play!"

That is life in the world today,
Outside the ole ball park,
For the lasting help and faith each play,
Thanks, Dad. Love, Mark

In Memory of Earnest Jefferson Wilkerson
7/7/29–8/9/88

"Quality Is the Mother…and We Don't Mess with Mom"

We embraced this quality motto early on at Successories, and I was greatly influenced by my creative partner and friend, Michael McKee. Our paper stock, our color separations, our frames, even our shipping cartons were of the highest quality. It was one of our core values.

I recall an incident in 1988 when we were at about $5 million in sales. Cash was tight, and we were watching every penny. Michael brought a copy of a new print into my office. It had just come off the press. As we were congratulating each other, my assistant walked in and pointed to an apostrophe in the quote at the bottom of the print. It should have come before the *S* instead of behind it.

Michael and I sat there stunned, because to reprint it would cost approximately $5,000, which we didn't have at the time. Although we both knew that 999 people out of 1,000 wouldn't notice the misplaced apostrophe, our commitment to quality gave us only one choice—destroy the prints and start over. It was a gut-wrenching decision, given our financial situation, but it was the right one. It left no doubt with our team that we were willing to walk the talk when it came to quality.

"Quality is never an accident; it is always the result of high intention, sincere effort, intelligent direction, and skillful execution; it represents the wise choice of many alternatives."

—*William A. Foster*

Know the Power of One Page

Joe Calhoon and Bruce Jeffrey are consultants who specialize in helping companies create a simple one-page strategic plan. I love the idea because there is something magic about one page. Here are the six key elements of the plan:

Vision: a clear picture of your destination

Mission: the driving purpose of your business

Values: the guide you use for decision-making and how you treat one another

Objectives: the numbers you track

Strategies: the paths you've decided to take

Priorities: the work that needs to get done and who needs to do it

According to Calhoon and Jeffrey, they've never seen a business plan that was too short, but they have seen hundreds that would make an acceptable cure for insomnia. They also said that once the management team understands the process, they have never encountered a company that couldn't fit their plan on one page. Does it take a little more time to drill down? Sure it does, but it's well worth it, because it forces you to cut out a lot of verbiage and make decisions on what's most important.

I love Blaise Pascal's quote: "I have made this longer than usual because I have not had time to make it shorter."

Take the time. You and your team will be glad you did.

"Focus on the critical few, and not the insignificant many."

—*Anonymous*

Even Eagles Need a Push

The eagle gently coaxed her offspring toward the edge of the nest. Her heart quivered with conflicting emotions as she felt their resistance to her persistent nudging. "Why does the thrill of soaring have to begin with the fear of falling?" she thought. This ageless question remained unanswered for her.

As in the tradition of the species, her nest was located high on the shelf of a sheer rock face. Below there was nothing but air to support the wings of each child. "Is it possible that this time it will not work?" she thought. Despite her fears, the eagle knew it was time. Her parental mission was all but complete. There remained one final task—the push.

The eagle drew courage from an innate wisdom. Until her children discovered their wings, there was no purpose for their lives. Until they learned how to soar, they would fail to understand the privilege it was to have been born an eagle. The push was the greatest gift she had to offer. It was her supreme act of love. And so, one by one, she pushed them—and they flew.

My friend David McNally wrote these words in his book *Even Eagles Need a Push*.

It's human nature to take the path of least resistance. Although most people truly want to reach their full potential, they don't always have the initiative and the discipline to get started on their own. One of your greatest responsibilities as a leader is to enable your people to be all they can be. Many times, the push, with a little encouragement, is all they need. Always look for opportunities to challenge your best people because many of them are like sticks of dynamite: the power's on the inside, but nothing happens until the fuse gets lit.

"You never know when a moment and a few sincere words can have an impact on a life."

—*Zig Ziglar*

Burn Brightly without Burning Out

Jim Cathcart is a friend and a great speaker. To manage your energy, Jim feels you need to find the pace at which you perform best. This is the zone in which you are most creative, unstressed, happy, and productive. He defines the zones as follows:

Above the zone: First, you experience stress and frustration, then anxiety, and finally burnout. At this level, you are overwhelming yourself with too many things to accomplish at one time. Lighten up a bit to get back on track.

In the zone: You are at your best. Not stressed, going with the flow of work naturally, productive and self-assured, challenged but not overwhelmed, motivated and able to roll with problems.

Below the zone: First, you experience boredom, then apathy, and finally depression. You feel useless and artificial; self-esteem suffers. Bite off more, and take greater challenges to get back on track.

Protecting and replenishing your emotional energy is critical for every leader. Mira Kirshenbaum, in her book *The Emotional Energy Factor*, offers some suggestions that are easy to implement. "First, you plug the leaks: learn to recognize what drains your energy—life situations, toxic people, or habits of mind like worry, guilt, indecision, and envy—and take steps to minimize it. Second, you identify what fills your tank—pleasure, prayer, novelty, anticipation, fun—and give yourself more."

"Things which matter most must never be at the mercy of things which matter least."

—*Johann Wolfgang von Goethe*

Turn Up the Fun-O-Meter

In his book *Rock Solid Leadership*, Robin Crow writes about visiting his sister, Laura, who worked for Southwest Airlines. He wrote:

> When we entered the building, which is home to over three thousand employees, I noticed over the elevator, etched in glass, was the Southwest Airlines mission statement: "The mission of Southwest Airlines is dedication to the highest quality of Customer Service delivered with a sense of warmth, friendliness, individual pride, and Company Spirit."
>
> Nothing too unusual about that, except for the fact it didn't even mention planes. Then, as I walked off the elevator onto the second floor, I was overwhelmed by these endless hallways, which were filled with thousands of pictures. I wish you could

have been there. There were photos of employees at charity ball games, Christmas parties, and company picnics. There were letters from celebrities and business competitors. There were articles and clippings about Southwest, as well as posters and brochures from the early days when the airline was just getting started.

According to Robin, here's the story…

When Southwest Airlines built their headquarters[...] they decided to fill their walls with photos and memorabilia. President Colleen Barrett (known as the "heart" of the company) began the tradition of asking employees to submit their own mementos to represent their personal lives and their experiences at Southwest.

The result is basically an enormous company scrapbook. I saw a cheerleading uniform, an old flight attendant uniform, and my favorite—a crushed tuba (although it did make me think twice about checking my guitar as luggage)—all matted and framed behind glass.

Each picture is a piece of what makes Southwest Airlines one of the most extraordinary companies in the world. These halls went on seemingly forever. Imagine, it's a five-story building, and those photos are on every level, floor to ceiling. There was one hallway completely devoted to photos of employees and their pets.

It was like the Smithsonian of employee appreciation. But as I started looking more closely at the photos, I noticed that most of them included at least one picture with Herb [Kelleher, the CEO] hanging out with that employee at a staff picnic or some other celebration—always laughing and having a great time.

It became so obvious to me that Herb's enthusiasm and spirit of celebration is at the core of what Southwest stands for as a company. And let me tell you, at Southwest, they know how to celebrate. They know the importance of having fun at work.

Laura says that it's not uncommon to see a spontaneous parade marching through headquarters in the middle of a busy workday or to see a department playing a game of hacky sack in the hallway or testing out their long jump skills. As all this was sinking in, I began to understand why Southwest's mission statement focused on "Customer Service, individual pride, and Company Spirit" over talking about airplanes. Southwest Airlines is all about people serving people.

The Results

While some of America's mammoth airlines are filing bankruptcy, Southwest is thriving and in the black. In fact, they have celebrated forty-two consecutive years of profitability.

So, one more time…turn up your fun-o-meter! Having fun with your team creates a magical bond like nothing else you can do.

"People rarely succeed unless they have fun in what they are doing."

—*Dale Carnegie*

The ONE Thing That Changes Everything

There is one thing that is common to every individual, team, family, organization, nation, economy, and civilization throughout the world—one thing which, if removed, will destroy the most powerful government, the most successful business, the most thriving economy, the most influential leadership, the greatest friendship, the strongest character, the deepest love.

On the other hand, if developed and leveraged, that one thing has the potential to create unparalleled success and prosperity in every dimension of life. Yet, it is the least understood, most neglected, and most underestimated possibility of our time.

That one thing is trust[...]

Contrary to what most people believe, trust is not some soft, illusive quality that you either have or you don't; rather, trust is a pragmatic, tangible, actionable asset that you can create—much faster than you probably think possible.

While corporate scandals, terrorist threats, office politics, and broken relationships have created low trust on almost every front, I contend that the ability to establish, grow, extend, and restore trust is not only vital to our personal and interpersonal well-being; it is the key leadership competency of the new global economy.

I am also convinced that in every situation, nothing is as fast as the speed of trust. And, contrary to popular belief, trust is something you can do something about. In fact, you can get good at creating it!

These words were written by Stephen M. R. Covey in the introduction of his book *The Speed of Trust*. Like the air we breathe, we too often take this critical intangible for granted. I urge you to read Covey's book. It helps every leader to truly understand how trust is the foundation for any true and lasting success.

"Trust men and they
will be true to you;
treat them greatly
and they will show
themselves great."

—*Ralph Waldo Emerson*

Know the Power of Humility

I've lived in Chicago for many years, and as you might expect, I'm a huge Chicago Bears fan. A few years ago, I got to watch one man emerge as the leader of the team. His name...Brian Urlacher. No question, Urlacher was a very talented football player. He had eight Pro Bowl seasons in his thirteen-year NFL career. But if you're a football fan, you know there are a lot of very talented football players who never become the unquestioned leader of their team.

Why is that? Obviously, there are many reasons a leader can emerge from the pack, but in Urlacher's case, it was his humility and his passion for the game.

I must say, for a superstar athlete, his humility was beyond refreshing. He never talked about himself, his achievements, his statistics, but he was always the first to praise and defend his teammates and his coaches.

When asked how he wanted to be remembered, he said, "Number one, I want to be remembered as a great teammate. As a guy who played hard and loved football."

When asked about his success in the NFL, he said, "I think I've adjusted pretty well, thanks to good coaches and great teammates. I won't say that I'm lucky, but just fortunate, I guess… I'm very blessed."

So many times, the difference in a good leader versus a great leader is one word—*humility*. A great leader is never afraid to poke fun at himself and is always first to give all the due credit to others.

"Humility is not
thinking less
of yourself,
it's thinking of
yourself less."

—*Rick Warren*

If You Chase Two Rabbits, Both Will Escape

At Successories in 1997, I learned about the power of focus the hard way. I didn't focus—and I paid the price. Golf was the hot sport because Tiger Woods had just come on the scene. We decided to purchase a small catalog company called British Links, a leader in golf art and golf gifts. The logic was simple:

1. We understood the specialty catalog business and were already mailing twenty million catalogs a year.
2. We understood the wall decor/framing business. Successories had become one of the largest framers in the country, and half of British Links's sales were from framed wall decor.

I won't bore you with the details of why this venture flopped, but within three years, we sold the golf company for next to nothing. However, the most devastating part of the deal was not the money we lost from the sale of British Links, but the momentum we had lost growing Successories, our core business.

In hindsight, I was an idiot! It was like Ray Kroc saying, after having opened twenty McDonald's, it's time to get into the pizza business. Many other businesses—like Starbucks and FedEx—focused their way to success. Repeat after me: less is more, less is more…

"In business,
real discipline
comes in saying
no to the wrong
opportunities."

—*Jim Collins*

Communicate, Communicate, Communicate

In her book *The Truth about Being a Leader*, Dr. Karen Otazo says there are three keys to effective communication:

1. **What's happening:** Share as much as you can about the company's goals and current projects, especially any good news, but also be proactive if things aren't going as planned.

2. **What's coming up:** This is a bit like "coming attractions." Your team is always interested in what's new.

3. **How they're doing:** This one is critical. Look for opportunities, private and public, to say good things or to talk about how they could do better. Most people want to know how they're doing but are afraid to ask. It is very important to visit and connect with team members personally.

YOU CAN'T SEND A DUCK TO EAGLE SCHOOL

The great leader truly understands that effective communication is the key that unlocks the door to trust.

"The single biggest problem in communication is the illusion that it has taken place."

—*George Bernard Shaw*

Luck Is Partly the Residue of Design

Bestselling author Harry Beckwith told me the following about luck:

> *For years in our work, we have preached the value of velocity. Successful companies succeed because they move, just as the individuals within them move too. At first these companies and these people seem lucky. So often they are in the right place at the right time. But they weren't in one place. They were in several—and one turned out to be right. They realized that luck was out there, and the key was getting into its path. Not certain which path luck might be on, these people chose several, and luck collided with them.*

YOU CAN'T SEND A DUCK TO EAGLE SCHOOL

For many years, Darrel Royal was the football coach for the University of Texas at Austin. They always had great teams and winning records. Sometimes, however, when they won a close game, a sportswriter would suggest that while the Longhorns were skilled, they had been lucky on that day. Hearing it one time too often, Coach Royal finally said, "Luck is partly the residue of design, the simple act of being prepared for luck when it arrives." And there is something else to luck, Royal said—luck follows speed.

Move, and luck finds you. Move quickly, and it finds you more often.

"It's tempting to sit and wait for life to come to you. But it can't. It's too busy. Life is out there. You have to go for it."

—*Harry Beckwith*

Patience Is Bitter, but the Fruit Can Be Sweet

Leo Tolstoy said, "The two most powerful warriors are patience and time."

If I had read that quote twenty-five years ago, it would have meant little to me. But today, I have a few business battle scars that easily could have been avoided had I listened to what Tolstoy said.

Some years ago, I had a speaking engagement in Hawaii. I arrived about midnight, and a driver met me at the airport to take me to my hotel. He was a young man with a real passion for life. On the way to the hotel, he shared his love for surfing. I asked him if it was dangerous, and he said, "Very dangerous, if you don't know what you're doing." He said that many people drown when a large wave takes them under, and instincts tell them to fight to get back to the surface. The key, he said, is to do just the opposite: let your body go limp, and the currents will bring you to the surface.

As a leader, there are times to act, and there are times to wait for the right answers to surface. Remember the quote from the very wise man Benjamin Franklin: "He that can have patience can have what he will."

"Patience is the best remedy for every trouble."

—*Plautus*

Know the Magic of Pulling Together

Not long ago, a friend sent me the story of Old Warwick. It brought a smile to my face, and I think it shares a wonderful lesson for every leader to learn.

A man was lost while driving through the country. As he tried to reach for the map, he accidentally drove off the road into a ditch. Though he wasn't injured, his car was stuck deep in the mud. So the man walked to a nearby farm to ask for help.

"Warwick can get you out of that ditch," said the farmer, pointing to an old mule standing in a field. The man looked at the decrepit old mule and looked at the farmer, who just stood there repeating, "Yep, old Warwick can do the job."

The man figured he had nothing to lose. The two men and the mule made their way back to the ditch. The farmer hitched the mule to the car. With a snap of the reins he shouted, "Pull, Fred! Pull, Jack! Pull, Ted! Pull, Warwick!" And the mule pulled that car right out of the ditch.

The man was amazed. He thanked the farmer, patted the mule, and asked, "Why did you call out all of those names before you called Warwick?"

The farmer grinned and said, "Old Warwick is just about blind. As long as he believes he's part of a team, he doesn't mind pulling."

Adapted from *Some Folks Feel the Rain, Others Just Get Wet* by James W. Moore

Teamwork is the ability to work together toward a common vision. The ability to direct individual accomplishment toward organizational objectives. It is the fuel that allows common people to attain uncommon results."

—*Andrew Carnegie*

Recognition Is a Need We All Crave

Dr. Abraham Maslow, one of the founders of modern psychology, said this: "Recognition is a need we all crave, and there are no exceptions." One of your greatest challenges as a manager is how to help your people fill this need.

Use your imagination for a few seconds. Pretend that you are in a football game. You're in the end zone waiting for the opening kickoff. You see the ball floating through the air, and you step up to catch it on the two yard line. You head for the middle of the field; you dodge a couple of tacklers; you cut right and head down the sidelines for ninety-eight yards. You reach the end zone, hands in the air. You turn around and...nothing. Not a sound. Your teammates are just strolling off the field. You think, *What happened? Did I run the wrong way?* But there are no boos. You think, *Something feels terribly wrong!*

But you know what? That's how it feels in many homes and workplaces every day. Somebody does something great, and they hear absolutely nothing.

Mario Fernandez said it best: "The human spirit is nurtured by praise, as much as a seedling is nurtured by the soil, the water, and the sun."

"The greatest management principle in the world is: 'the things that get rewarded and appreciated get done.'"

—*Michael LeBoeuf*

Identify Your Core Values

There are two things I believe with all my heart:

1. Core values are critical to build great brands and great companies.
2. They must be continuously enforced to truly make it a part of your company culture.

Why the need for values in an organization? Core values serve as critical guides for making decisions, and when in doubt, they cut through the fog like a beacon in the night.

Identifying the core values that define your company is one of the more important functions of leadership. They can make or break your long-term success. But you also should know that gaps between your values and your actions can do more harm than good. In other words, if you talk about building a customer-first culture but fail to do so, you'll lose the respect of your employees and your customers.

Therefore, as a leader, you must select your core values carefully, because once you commit, your credibility is on the line.

"Goals are for the future; values are for now. Goals are set; values are lived. Goals change; values are rocks that you can count on."

—*Sheldon Bowles*

Walk Your Talk

A while back, I was invited to spend some time with Ken Blanchard at his lake home in upstate New York. Over the last twenty years, Ken has probably sold more books than any other business author. His classic, *The One Minute Manager,* has sold over ten million copies. He has also built a large training company with the focus on servant leadership and customer service.

I've had the good fortune to meet many successful businessmen, authors, and speakers during my career, but I've never met anyone who walked the talk more than Ken. He gets it.

The first night of my visit to Ken's lake home, we were sitting on the deck with Humberto, his son-in-law, talking about some ways we could work together. It was about 10:00 p.m. when, all of a sudden, Ken jumped up and asked to be excused. He returned about 10:20 p.m., and Humberto asked, "What happened?" Ken said, "I can't believe it. I forgot to call Dorothy on her birthday."

Later that night, after Ken had gone to bed, Humberto told me that Dorothy is an eighty-five-year-old, part-time employee for the company. It then dawned on me that at 10:00 p.m., Ken left to spend almost twenty minutes talking to Dorothy and inquiring about how she had spent her special day. However, after spending more time with Ken over the next year, I came to realize that this was no fluke. This is who he is. One time, while visiting him at his San Diego office, I learned that one of his employees who worked in the warehouse had recently passed away. On that day, Ken had invited the employee's wife to come to his office. When she arrived, he spent an hour walking around with her, carrying a tape recorder to record all of the wonderful memories other employees had of her husband. When the wife left, she said it was a day she'd never forget.

You see, what many leaders would have considered a waste of time, Ken saw as an opportunity to serve and to thank his people. He doesn't do it because it's expected of him; he does it because he truly cares. It comes from his heart, and his people love him for being the servant leader that he is.

This is an old Chinese poem that offers wonderful advice for any leader:

Go to the people,
Live among them,
Learn from them,
Love them.
Start with what they know,
Build on what they have:
But of the best leaders,
When their task is accomplished,
Their work is done,
The people all remark,
"We have done it ourselves."

About the Author

Mac Anderson is the founder of Simple Truths and Successories, Inc., the leader in designing and marketing products for motivation and recognition. These companies, however, are not the first success stories for Mac. He was also the founder and CEO of McCord Travel, the largest travel company in the Midwest, and part owner/vice president of sales and marketing for Orval Kent Food Company, the country's largest manufacturer of prepared salads.

His accomplishments in these unrelated industries provide some insight into his passion and leadership skills. He also brings the same passion when speaking to many corporate audiences on a variety of topics, including leadership, motivation, and team building.